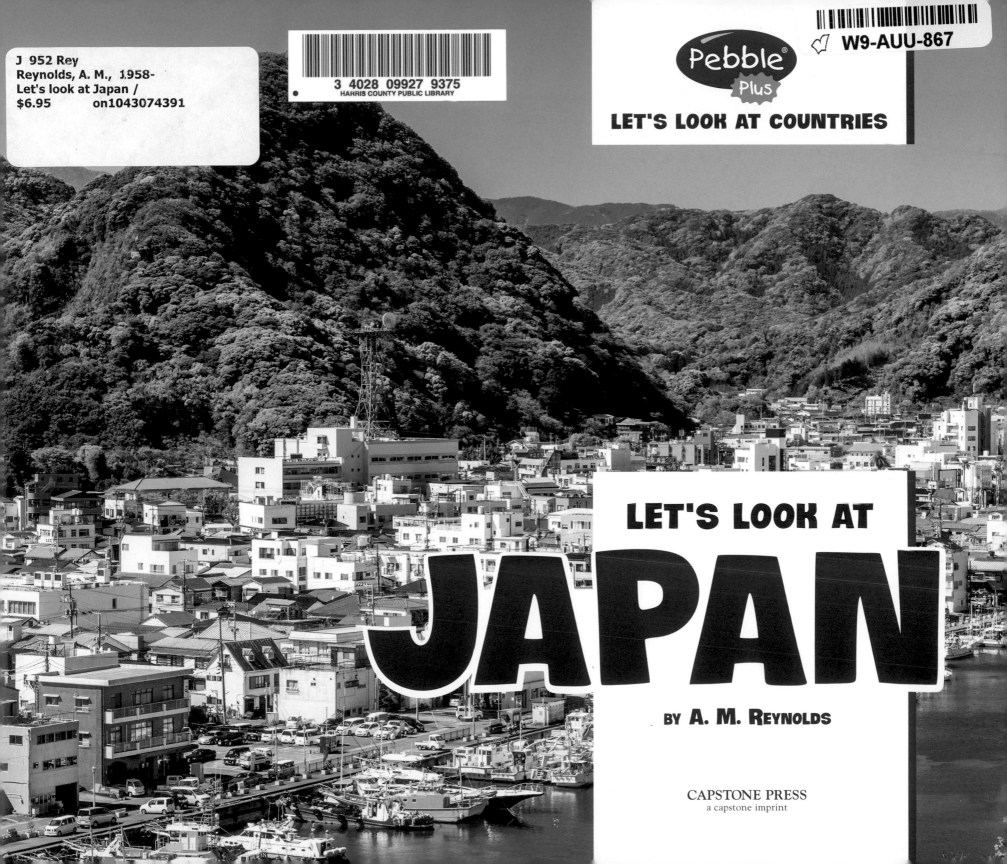

Pebble® Plus

LET'S LOOK AT COUNTRIES

LET'S LOOK AT JAPAN

BY A. M. REYNOLDS

CAPSTONE PRESS
a capstone imprint

Pebble Plus is published by Capstone Press,
1710 Roe Crest Drive, North Mankato, Minnesota 56003
www.mycapstone.com

Library of Congress Cataloging-in-Publication Data
Names: Reynolds, A. M., 1958– author.
Title: Let's look at Japan / by A.M. Reynolds.
Description: North Mankato, Minnesota : Capstone Press, 2019. | Series: Pebble plus. Let's look at
countries
Identifiers: LCCN 2018029937 (print) | LCCN 2018031715 (ebook) | ISBN 9781977103932 (eBook
PDF) | ISBN 9781977103840 (hardcover) | ISBN 9781977105639 (pbk.)
Subjects: LCSH: Japan—Juvenile literature.
Classification: LCC DS806 (ebook) | LCC DS806 .R368 2019 (print) | DDC 952—dc23
LC record available at https://lccn.loc.gov/2018029937

Editorial Credits
Erika L. Shores, editor; Juliette Peters, designer; Jo Miller, media researcher;
Laura Manthe, production specialist

Photo Credits
Getty Images: kokouu, 17; Newscom: Pictures From History/William Ng, 10; Shutterstock:
501room, 15, anuar.mohammad, 21, Blue Planet Studio, Cover Top, cowardlion, 14, f11photo, 5,
Globe Turner, 22 (Inset), gontabunta, 13, KPG Payless2, Cover Middle, Martin Voeller, 8, nate, 4,
panparinda, 9, Perati Komson, 11, Sean Pavone, 1, 3, shikema, 22-23, 24, Shuttertong, Cover Bottom,
Cover Back, tororo reaction, 7, Vincent St. Thomas, 19

Note to Parents and Teachers

The Let's Look at Countries set supports national curriculum standards for social studies related
to people, places, and culture. This book describes and illustrates Japan. The images support early
readers in understanding the text. The repetition of words and phrases helps early readers learn
new words. This book also introduces early readers to subject-specific vocabulary words, which are
defined in the Glossary section. Early readers may need assistance to read some words and to use
the Table of Contents, Glossary, Read More, Internet Sites, Critical Thinking Questions, and Index
sections of the book.

Printed and bound in China.
970

TABLE OF CONTENTS

Where Is Japan?

Japan is an island country in eastern Asia. It is nearly as big as the U.S. state of California. Japan's capital is Tokyo.

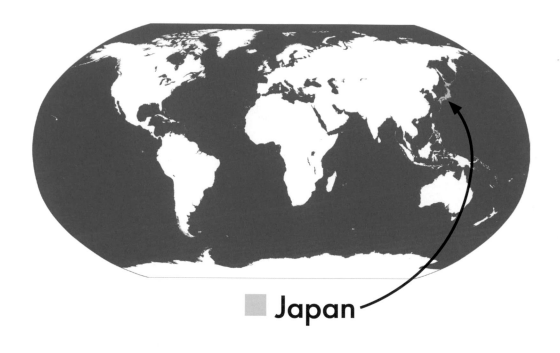

Japan

Tokyo, Japan

From Mountains to the Seas

The Pacific Ocean circles Japan.

Japan has four main islands.

The country also has more than

6,800 smaller islands. Mountains and

forests cover much of these islands.

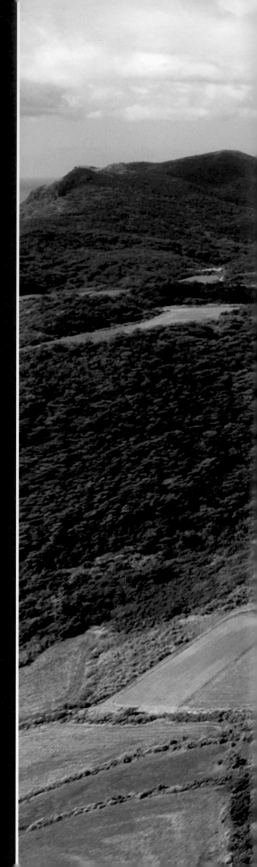

In the Wild

Japan's forests are home to bears and deer. Monkeys and flying squirrels climb the trees. Japanese giant salamanders swim in streams.

giant salamander

snow monkeys

People

People have lived in Japan
for more than 10,000 years.
Most people live in cities
on the coasts. Japan has
an emperor who is like a king.

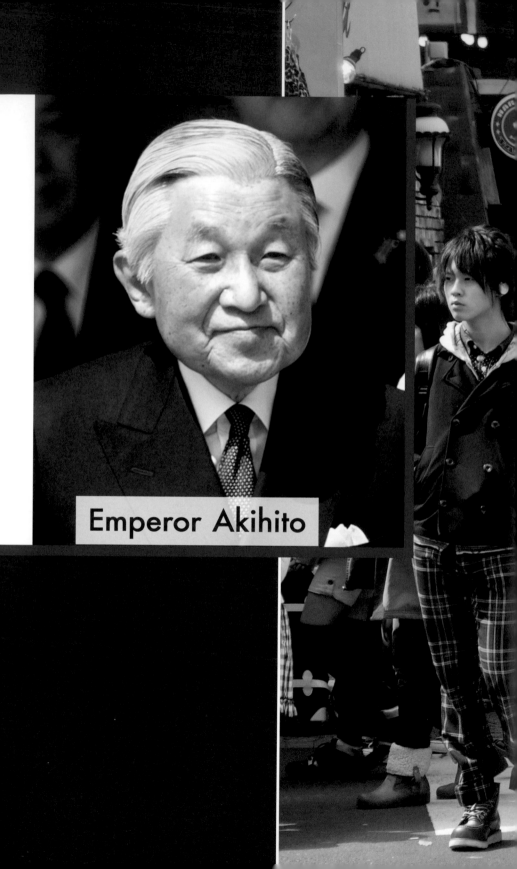

Emperor Akihito

At the Table

Japanese eat healthy food.

They eat fish, rice,

and vegetables. Sushi and

rice crackers are snack foods.

Festivals

Japan celebrates spring with the Cherry Blossom Festival. People meet their friends and picnic under the trees. They enjoy the cherry blossoms.

On the Job

Most Japanese work in service jobs.

They work in stores, banks, and offices.

People make cars and electronics

in factories. Other Japanese are

farmers and fishers.

Transportation

People in Japan travel by plane,

car, bus, and train.

Railroads lead all over Japan.

People ride on very fast trains

called bullet trains.

Famous Site

Visitors come to Japan to see Mount Fuji. Some people climb 12,389 feet (3,766 meters) to the top. It is an active volcano.

QUICK JAPAN FACTS

Japanese flag

Name: Japan
Capital: Tokyo
Other major cities: Osaka, Nagoya, and Sapporo
Population: 126,451,398 (2017 estimate)
Size: 145,914 square miles (377,915 sq km)
Language: Japanese
Money: Japanese Yen

GLOSSARY

active volcano—currently erupting or likely to erupt

bullet train—a high speed train that travels faster than 200 miles (320 kilometers) per hour

capital—the city or town in a country where the government is based

emperor—a male leader who is the symbol of the country's customs and beliefs

flying squirrel—a type of squirrel that can glide between branches of trees

giant salamander—the second largest amphibian in the world

sushi—a small rice roll wrapped in nori (seaweed)

READ MORE

Blevins, Wiley. *Japan.* Follow Me Around. New York: Scholastic, 2018.

Mattern, Joanne. *Japan.* Exploring World Cultures. New York: Cavendish Square, 2019.

Nakaya, Andrea C. *Growing Up in Japan.* Growing Up Around the World. San Diego, Calif.: ReferencePoint Press, 2018.

INTERNET SITES

Use FactHound to find Internet sites related to this book.

Visit *www.facthound.com*

Just type 9781977103840 and go.

Check out projects, games and lots more at
www.capstonekids.com

CRITICAL THINKING QUESTIONS

1. Why is Japan called a chain of islands?

2. Describe some of the foods people eat in Japan.

3. Can you name some types of electronics?

INDEX